The month of April, from the illuminated manuscript
Les Très Riches Heures du duc de Berry

The Story of a Special Day
Volume 103

April 12

102nd day of the year
(103rd in leap years)
263 days remaining
until the end of the year.

by Michael Dobson

Timespinner Press

Table of Contents

Cover: Mockup of Vostok-1 capsule in the Musée de l'Air et de l'Espace, Paris, whch flew Yuri Gagarin on the first human flight into outer space, April 12, 1961 — the *Event of the Day.*

Back Cover and Frontispiece: The month of April, from the French Gothic illuminated manuscript *Les Très Riches Heures du duc de Berry.*

April 12 Quotations

"Even if you win the rat race, you're still a rat."

—William Sloane Coffin, died April 12, 2006

"Sacred cows make the tastiest hamburger."

—Abbie Hoffman, died April 12, 1989

"He can run, but he can't hide."

—Joe Louis, died April 12, 1981

"Next in importance to having a good aim is to recognize when to pull the trigger."

—David Letterman, born April 12, 1947

"Wars are begun by frightened men. They fear war, but more than that, they fear what will happen if they don't start one."

—Tom Clancy, born April 12, 1947

"I don't care who does the electing, so long as I get to do the nominating."

—William "Boss" Tweed, died April 12, 1978

"All religions united with government are more or less inimical to liberty. All, separated from government, are compatible with liberty.

—Henry Clay, born April 12, 1777

Event of the Day
First Manned Spaceflight

Yuri Gagarin on the way to the launch pad

On April 12, 1961, the Russian Vostok-1 (Восток-1) spacecraft, carrying cosmonaut Yuri Gagarin, lifted off from Baikonur Cosmodrome in Kazakhstan and completed one full orbit around the earth. This was the first time a human being went into outer space and the first time a manned vehicle completed an orbit of the Earth.

The Soviet Union had successfully launched the first artificial satellite, Sputnik-1 (Спутник-1) in 1957. ("Sputnik" simply means "Satellite.") This caused what was described as a "wave of near-hysteria" in the United States, as Americans generally regarded the Soviet Union as a backward country at the time. The United States embarked on a huge technological research program, known as the "Space Race," to catch up.

The Soviets launched additional satellites and unmanned missions, with variable success, before they felt ready for a manned flight. Security was so high that even the name of the project director was classified, known only in the West as the "Chief Designer." His real name, Sergei Pavlovich Korolev (Серге́й Па́влович Королёв), was only revealed to the public after his death in 1966.

The cosmonaut for the Vostok-1 mission ("Vostok" means "East" or "Orient") was chosen only four days before the launch: 27-year old Yuri Alekseyevich Gagarin (Ю́рий Алексе́евич Гага́рин). His Soviet Air Force file described him as "modest; embarrasses when humor gets a little too racy; high degree of intellectual development; fantastic memory; quick reactions; persevering; excels in higher mathematics." Gagarin was also the choice of his fellow cosmonauts in a secret ballot.

Launch occured at 06:07 UT (Universal Time; 9:07am Moscow time). Because no one was certain at the time how the human body would react to weightlessness, the mission was fully automated. Two minutes into the flight, the four strap-on booster sections fell away, followed three minutes later by the rocket core stage.

Orbit was achieved at 06:17 UT, and at 07:25 UT, the automated systems aligned the capsule for reentry. The Vostok service module was supposed to separate from the man-carrying capsule, but a bundle of wires interfered, and both halves of the spacecraft reentered the atmosphere.

The capsule gyrated strongly. Gagarin telegraphed "Everything is OK" rather than report the problem, and indeed that turned out to be the case when the wires broke and the service module fell away.

Unlike American spacecraft that touched down in the ocean, Vostok-1 would touch down on land. Rather than risk an accident at touchdown, Gagarin ejected at an altitude of seven kilometers (23,000 feet) and parachuted down. The parachute on the capsule deployed successfully at 2.5km (8,200 ft).

Gagarin landed about ten minutes later; both he and the spaceship touched down about 280km to the west of the planned landing site. A farmer and her daughter were the first to see Gagarin upon landing. Gagarin said, "When they saw me in my space suit...they started to back away in fear. I told them, don't be afraid...I must find a telephone to call Moscow!"

The official rules set by the Fédération Aéronautique Internationale (FAI) for record-setting flights required that the pilot land with the spaceship to be considered an official spaceflight, so the Soviet Union officially declared that he had done so, only admitting the truth in 1971. They also lied about the location of the launch site to keep it a secret. Today, the Vostok-1 capsule is in the RKK Energiya museum near Moscow.

Although the United States eventually won the space race on July 21, 1969, when the Apollo 11 mission reached the Moon, Gagarin's record as the first human in space is unassailable. In Russia and other former USSR countries, April 12 is celebrated as Cosmonautics Day (День Космонавтики) to commemorate this achievement.

Additional space milestones have taken place on April 12. The first orbital test flight of the Space Shuttle took place on the 20th anniversary of the Vostok-1 launch, when *Columbia* took off for the STS-1 mission. (Earlier Shuttle test flights did not go into space.)

April 12 has also been declared the International Day of Human Space Flight by the United Nations. In 2001, the 40th anniversary of the mission, Americans involved in spaceflight created "Yuri's Night," a celebration of space exploration milestones.

Yuri's Night celebrations have taken place in Los Angeles, Huntsville, New Orleans, Stockholm, Tel Aviv, Tokyo, Afghanistan, Latvia, Peru, Antarctica, and on the International Space Station, with celebrities including Ray Bradbury and Nichelle Nichols (*Uhura* from Star Trek).

Yuri Gagarin died in a plane crash in 1968.

April 12 Holidays and Celebrations

Halifax Day (North Carolina)

On April 12, 1776, the North Carolina Provincial Congress, meeting in Halifax, North Carolina, adopted the "Halifax Resolves," the first official declaration urging independence for the American colonies, which helped pave the way for the Declaration of Independence. April 12 is celebrated in Historic Halifax with Revolutionary War reenactors and others in period costumes.

Cerealia (ancient Rome)

The Cerealia in ancient rome was a seven-day festival in honor of the grain goddess Ceres. Rituals included tying blazing torches to the tails of live foxes and releasing them in the Circus Maximus, along with a horse race and theatrical performances.

National Drop Everything and Read (D.E.A.R.) Day (United States)

D.E.A.R. Day promotes sustained silent reading among students. It is celebrated on April 12, the birthday of noted children's author Beverly Cleary (see "Who Was Born on April 12?").

Easter Season

Easter is a "moveable feast," meaning it occurs on different days each year. In Western Christianity, Easter can occur anywhere between March 22 and April 25; in Eastern Christianity it can occur anywhere from April 4 to May 8. (The difference is that Eastern Christianity calculates according to the older Julian calendar rather than the modern Gregorian calendar. See "What Day of the Week is April 11?" for an explanation.) All events of the Easter season adjust accordingly. See the "Easter Events" section for more details.

Christian Feast Days

In **Western Christianity**, April 12 is the feast day of Alferius, Blessed Angelo Carletti di Chivasso, Erkembode, Pope Julius I, and Zeno of Verona.

In **Eastern Orthodox Christianity**, April 12 is the also the commemoration of Zeno of Verona, along with Saint Basil the Confessor; Virgin Anthusa of Constantinople; Saint Athanasia of Aegina; the martyrs Menas, David, and John of Palestine; Saint Isaac of Monteluco; martyr Acacius of Kapsokalvyvia Skete; Saint Basil of Ryazan, and martyrs Demas, Prorion, and those with them. It is also the Deposition of the Belt of the Most Holy Mother of God in Constantinople. (These events are observed on April 25 by "Old Calendarists" who use the Julian calendar.)

What Happened on April 12?

1204 CE – **Sack of Constantinople**

Seeking revenge for the Massacre of the Latins in 1182, the Fourth Crusade had as its objective the destruction of Constantinople, capital of the Byzantine Empire. The Siege of Constantinople by Crusaders began in March 1204, and in spite of attempts by the Byzantine Empire to negotiate terms, the Crusaders began their assault on the walls of the city on April 9. Bad weather and heavy archery fire worked against the Crusaders at first, but on April 12, 1204, the Crusaders were able to seize some of the guard towers and began to knock holes in the walls.

The Crusaders burned down a large part of the city, leaving 15,000 homeless, and looted and vandalized the city for three days. They destroyed a number of ancient and medieval Roman and Greek statues, the Library of Constantinople, churches, monasteries and convents. Thousands were killed, raped, and brutalized, and Constantinople was divided between the Republic of Venice and various Crusader leaders, establishing the Latin Empire of Constantinople.

1606 CE – **Britain Adopts the Union Jack**

When James VI of Scotland, son of Mary Queen of Scots, inherited the thrones of England and Ireland (as James I, because England had never had a King James) on the death of Elizabeth I, he united the three crowns. The flag of the new Union combined the English and Scottish flags into a single design. England's flag was a red cross on a white background, while Scotland's was a white saltire (an "x") on a blue background; the combined design was known either as the Union Flag or the Union Jack.

The current flag of the United Kingdom of Great Britain and Northern Ireland adds the Irish Saint Patrick's flag, a red saltire on a white background, forming the design we know today.

The modern Union Jack

1861 CE – **Attack on Fort Sumter**

After South Carolina declared its secession from the United States, Union forces moved into Fort Sumter, located on an island in Charleston Harbor. Confederate leaders demanded its surrender on April 11, 1861, and following a Union refusal, the Confederates began firing on the fort at 4:30am on Friday, April 12, 1861. The battle lasted until the following day, when the fort was surrendered and evacuated. The shots fired on Fort Sumter began the American Civil War.

Confederate batteries fire on Fort Sumter

1862 CE – **The Great Locomotive Chase**

Buster Keaton in *The General*

Andrew's Raid, often called the Great Locomotive Chase, began April 12, 1862, when Union volunteers commandeered a Confederate passenger train in Big Shanty (Kennesaw), Georgia, and drove it north toward Chattanooga, destroying the railway as they traveled, while being pursued by Confederate forces initially on foot and later by different locomotives. The raiders were eventually caught and most were hanged as spies. Andrew's Raid has been made into a film twice: Buster Keaton's classic silent film *The General*, and again by Walt Disney in 1956.

1864 CE – **Fort Pillow Massacre**

After Union forces captured and occupied Fort Pillow, near Memphis, Tennessee, Confederate forces commanded by Nathan Bedford Forrest overran the fort following a fierce battle. About half the Union soldiers were African-Americans; following the battle, Confederate troops massacred the surrendered black soldiers in what military historians have called "one of the bleakest, saddest events of American military history."

The Fort Pillow Masssacre became a rallying cry in the North, increasing Union determination to see the war through to its conclusion.

1937 CE – First Jet Engine

Whittle Jet Engine

RAF Pilot Officer Frank Whittle conceived of the jet engine in 1929, but encountered substantial resistance from the Air Ministry. Pushing ahead on his own, Whittle arranged for private financing for his idea, and on April 12, 1937, ran the first successful test of a jet engine. Although his successful test came earlier than German parallel efforts, the German Heinkel He 178 flew nine months before the British Gloster E. 28/39 using Whittle's designs.

1945 CE – FDR Dies; Truman Becomes President

After a long illness, President Franklin Delano Roosevelt died of a stroke in his retreat at Warm Springs, Georgia. Vice President Harry S. Truman, who had been in office for only 82 days, succeeded to the Presidency later the same day.

From left to right: FDR, Harry Truman,
former Vice President Henry Wallace

1955 CE – **First Polio Vaccine**

The disease of poliomyelitis has been a part of the human condition throughout history, but beginning in the 1880s, major epidemics of the disease broke out in Europe and the United States. At its peak, the disease paralyzed or killed over 500,000 people worldwide each year. An intense race to develop a vaccine against the disease finally succeeded when Dr. Jonas Salk announced his vaccine on April 12, 1955. Along with the oral vaccine developed by Dr. Alfred Sabin, this research has virtually eradicated polio in most countries.

1980 CE –
Marathon of Hope

After the amputation of his leg as a result of cancer, Canadian Terry Fox (right)resolved to make a cross-country run to raise money for cancer research. Beginning on April 12, 1980, he ran the equivalent of a full marathon each day on his artificial leg, but was forced to abandon the attempt after 143 days and over 5,000 kilometers (3,000 miles) when the

cancer spread to his lungs. He died nine months later. The annual Terry Fox Run in his honor now takes place in 60 countries and has raised over C$500 milion for cancer research in his name.

1980 CE – Coup in Libya

On April 12, 1980, Samuel Doe led a military coup d'état to take over the African nation of Liberia, which had been colonized beginning in 1820 with freed slaves from the United States. The decendents of those colonists were a minority in the country, but dominated the political and economic environment. Doe, part of a rural tribe, attempted to reverse the situation, but fraudulent elections and corruption led to loss of support and the outbreak of a series of civil wars that only ended in 2005 after the death of 200,000 Liberians and displacement of a million more.

1994 CE – Commercial Spamming Hits the Internet

On April 12, 1994, a massive commercial advertisement for "green card" services hit over 5,500 members of Usenet, the major part of the Internet before the popularity of the World Wide Web — at the time, a huge number for the still-nascent Internet culture. This was the first commercial Internet spam, and was propagated by a husband-and-wife legal team, Laurence Canter and Martha Siegel, were responsible. They are considered the beginning of the modern spamming industry.

1999 CE – Bill Clinton Cited for Contempt

Following his acquittal by the U. S. Senate in the Lewinsky scandal, President Bill Clinton was cited for civil contempt of court by Judge Susan Wright for giving "intentionally false statements" in the sexual harrassment lawsuit filed against him by Paula Jones. His law license was suspended for five years and he was fined $90,000.

Who Was Born on April 12?

Arts, Theatre, Literature

John Krakauer (April 12, 1954 —)

Krakauer's best-selling nonfiction books about mountain climbing include *Into the Wild* and *Into Thin Air.*

Scott Turow (April 12, 1949 —)

Turow's best-selling legal thrillers include 1987's *Presumed Innocent,* made into a 1990 film starrin Harrison Ford.

Tom Clancy (April 12, 1947 —)

Military thriller writer Tom Clancy's best-sellers include *The Hunt for Red October, Clear and Present Danger, Patriot Games,* and *Red Storm Rising.* Several of his books have been made into movies.

Alan Ayckbourn (April 12, 1939 —)

Over forty of Alan Ayckbourn's plays have been produced in London's West End and ten have been staged on Broadway. His plays include *Absurd Person Singular* and *The Norman Conquests* trilogy.

Beverly Cleary (April 12, 1916 —)

Children's author Cleary has sold 91 million copies of her books about Henry Huggins, Beezus and Ramona, and Ralph S. Mouse. She won the 1984 Newbery Medal and the 1981 National Book Award. D.E.A.R. Day (see "April 12 Holidays and Celebrations") is held on her birthday.

Hardie Gramatky (April 12, 1907 — April 29, 1979)

Named by Andrew Wyeth as one of America's greatest watercolorists, Gramatky is known today for his illustrated children's book Little Toot. His work is in the collections of the Whitney Museum of Art, the Metropolitan Museum of Art, and many other museums, and his work appeared in such magazines as *Fortune, Women's Day*, and *Reader's Digest.*

Felix de Weldon (April 12, 1907 — June 3, 2003)

Sculptor Felix de Weldon created over 1,200 sculptures displayed on seven continents in a long and distinguished career. His most famous work is the U. S. Marine Corps War Memorial (Iwo Jima Memorial) in Washington, DC.

The U. S. Marine Corps War Memorial,

José Gautier Benítez (April 12, 1851 — January 24, 1880)

Puerto Rican poet Benítez is honored as one of the commonwealth's best literary figures. Schools, libraries, and other institutions are named for him, and there is a statue of him in Caguas.

Alexander Nikolayevich Ostrovsky (Алекса́ндр Остро́вский)(April 12 [O.S. March 31], 1823 — June 14 [O.S. June 2], 1823)

Ostrovsky is considered the most important playwright of the Russian realistic period. His 47 plays are among the most frequently staged pieces in Russia.

Edward de Vere, 17th Earl of Oxford (April 12, 1550 — June 24, 1604)

Known in his time as a patron of the arts and a minor poet and playwright, Edward de Vere (left) is considered by "anti-Stratfordians" (people who doubt that Shakespeare wrote the plays and poems with which he is credited) as the leading alternate candidate.

Crime

Enedina Arellano Félix (April 12, 1961 —)

According to the DEA, Félix is the first female drug lord, heading the Tijuana Cartel following the arrest of her brother in 2008.

Henri Désiré Landru (April 12, 1869 — February 25, 1922)

French serial killer Landru placed advertisements in "lonely hearts" sections in Paris newspapers, lured widows to his villa, stole their money, and murdered them. He was convicted of eleven murders and was executed by guillotine. He was the inspiration for Charlie Chaplin's film *Monsieur Verdoux*, the subject of the 1960 film *Bluebeard's Ten Honeymoons*, and part of a *Twilight Zone* episode (as a wax figure), as well as other films. His severed head is on display at the Museum of Death in Hollywood

Film, Fashion and Television

Brooklyn Decker (April 12, 1987 —)

Swimwear model for Sports Illustrated and Victoria's Secret, Decker has appeared in numerous TV shows and movies, including featured roles in *Battleship* and *What to Expect When You're Expecting*.

Claire Danes (April 12, 1979 —)

Claire Danes came to fame in the TV series *My So-Called Life* and starred in the Showtime series *Homeland.*

Jennifer Morrison (April 12, 1979 —)

Television actress Morrison played Dr. Allison Cameron in *House* and Emma Swan in *Once Upon a Time.*

Marley Shelton (April 12, 1974 —)

Shelton had starring roles in the films *Sugar & Spice* and *A Perfect Getaway,* and was the lead in the CBS series *Eleventh Hour.*

Shannen Doherty (April 12, 1971 —)

Doherty's breakthrough role was as Brenda Walsh on the 1990s TV series *Beverly Hills, 90210.*

Nicholas Brendon (April 12, 1971 —)

Brendon played Xander on the TV series *Buffy the Vampire Slayer.*

Alice Coppola (April 12, 1968 —)

Coppola played IRS Agent Mimi Clark in *Jericho,* an FBI agent in *National Treasure: Book of Secrets,* and in guest roles in numerous other series. She began as a hostess on the game show *Remote Control.*

Magda Szubanski (April 12, 1961 —)

Szubanski played Esme in the 1995 film *Babe* and its sequel, and Furlow on the TV series *Farscape*.

Andy García (April 12, 1956 —)

García starred in *The Godfather Part III*, *The Untouchables*, and the *Ocean's Eleven* films. He was nominated for an Oscar for *The Godfather Part III*.

David Letterman (April 12, 1947 —)

Comedian David Letterman has had the longest late-night hosting career in television. Since 1982, he hosted *Late Night with David Letterman* on CBS. He founded a production company, Worldwide Pants, which produced the sitcom *Everybody Loves Raymond*.

Late Show with David Letterman theatre marquee in New York City

Dan Lauria (April 12, 1947 —)

Dan Lauria is best known as the father on the 1988-1993 TV series *The Wonder Years*.

Wayne Northrop (April 12, 1947 —)

Northrop appeared in soap operas including *Days of Our Lives* (as Roman Brady and Dr. Alex North) and *Dynasty*.

Ed O'Neill (April 12, 1946 —)

Ed O'Neill played Al Bundy on *Married… With Children* and Jay Pritchett on *Modern Family*.

Hardy Krüger (April 12, 1928 —)

German actor Krüger starred in a number of American films including the original *The Flight of the Phoenix*, *A Bridge Too Far*, *Hatari!*, and Stanley Kubrick's *Barry Lyndon*.

Ann Miller (April 12, 1923 — January 22, 2004)

Dancer and actress Ann Miller (left, in a World War II pinup) appeared in MGM musicals including *Easter Parade*, *On the Town*, and *Kiss Me Kate*. She is credited with popularizing pantyhose.

Walt Gorney (April 12, 1912 — March 5, 2004)

Actor Gorney is remembered for playing Crazy Ralph, the drunken old man who says "You're all doomed!" in the *Friday the 13th* film franchise.

Bobby Harron (April 12, 1869 — February 25, 1922)

Harron appeared on over 200 films during the silent era, including two classic D. W. Griffith films, *The Birth of a Nation* and *Intolerance*.

Harold Lockwood (April 12, 1887 — October 19, 1918)

Silent film star Lockwood was a matinee idol during the 1910s. He appeared in over 20 films, including the 1916 classic D. W. Griffith film *Intolerance*.

Military

Robert Lee Scott, Jr. (April 12, 1908 — February 27, 2006)

USAF General Scott wrote *God is My Co-Pilot* about his World War II service with the Flying Tigers in China and Burma.

Music

Mellow Man Ace (April 12, 1967 —)

As Mellow Man Ace and Lord Sha'mel Allah, rapper Ulpiano Sergio Reyes had a hit single with "Mentirosa," and was in the group Cypress Hill.

Vince Gill (April 12, 1957 —)

Country singer-songwriter Vince Gill's #1 hits include "I Still Believe in You," "One More Last Chance," and "Don't Let Our Love Start Slippin' Away." He was inducted into the Country Music Hall of Fame in 2007.

Pat Travers (April 12, 1947 —)

Canadian blues rock guitarist Pat Travers had a 1980's hit with "Snortin' Whiskey, Drinking Cocaine," featured in the 2004 movie *Sideways*.

David Cassidy (April 12, 1950 —)

Cassidy was a 1970s teen idol for his role as Keith in the TV sitcom *The Partridge Family*.

Alex Briley (April 12, 1947 —)

Alex Briley is the "G.I" in the disco group Village People. His brother Jonathan Briley has been identified as the "Falling Man" photographed falling from the World Trade Center on September 11, 2001.

John Kay (April 12, 1944 —)

Kay was the frontman for the rock group Steppenwolf, whose hits included "Born to Be Wild" and "Magic Carpet Ride."

Herbie Hancock (April 12, 1940 —)

Jazz fusion pianist and composer Herbie Hancock was a pioneer of the "post-bop" sound, and was one of the first jazz musicians to incorporate funk and soul. He scored the 1966 film *Blowup*, composed the soundtrack for the children's TV show *Fat Albert and the Cosby Kids*, and won 14 Grammys.

Tiny Tim (April 12, 1932 — November 30, 1996)

As "Tiny Tim," Herbert Khaury had a 1968 novelty hit with his rendition of "Tiptoe Through the Tulips" sung in a high falsetto while playing the ukulele. His breakthrough appearance on *Rowan and Martin's Laugh-In* led to a brief period of fame, culminating in his 1969 marriage to "Miss Vicki" on Johnny Carson's *Tonight Show*.

Billy Vaughn (April 12, 1919 — September 26, 1991)

Billy Vaughn reached the *Billboard* charts with 42 singles and 36 albums, and was a hit in Germany, India, New Zealand, Italy, Japan, and elsewhere. While he charted with "Wheels," "Sail Along Silv'ry Moon," and "A Swingin' Safari," among others.

Tiny Tim (center) on *Laugh-In*,
with Rowan (kneeling) and Martin (laughing)

Helen Forrest (April 12, 1917 — July 11, 1999)

Helen Forrest was the "girl singer" for the Artie Shaw, Benny Goodman, and Harry James big bands.

Russell Garcia (April 12, 1916 — November 19, 2011)

Composer and arranger Russell Garcia scored the TV series *Rawhide*, films including *The Time Machine* and *The Benny Goodman Story*, and worked for top musical and Hollywood stars from Ella Fitzgerald to Walt Disney and Ronald Reagan.

Hound Dog Taylor (April 12, 1915 — December 17, 1975)

Chicago blues guitarist and singer Theodore Roosevelt Taylor performed with such blues acts as Muddy Waters and Big Mama Thornton, and inspired George Thorogood. He is a member of the Blues Hall of Fame.

Lily Pons (April 12, 1898 — February 13, 1976)

Operatic soprano and actress Lily Pons (right) performed nearly 300 times with the Metropolitan Opera, made musicals for RKO Pictures, appeared on *The Ed Sullivan Show* and other television programs, and was in advertisements for Lockheed airplanes, Knox gelatin, and Libby's tomato juice.

Politics

William B. Bankhead (April 12, 1874 — September 15, 1940)

Alabama representative Bankhead served as Speaker of the House of Representatives and was a key supporter of FDR's New Deal legislation. He was the father of Tallulah Bankhead.

George N. Briggs (April 12, 1796 — September 12, 1861)

Briggs served seven terms as Governor of Massachusetts, the 19th person to hold that office. He also served in Congress. He was accidentally killed when serving on a diplomatic mission to South America on behalf of Abraham Lincoln.

Henry Clay (April 12, 1777 — June 29, 1852)

Kentucky senator and representative Henry Clay (left) was Speaker of the House three times, served as Secretary of State, and ran unsuccessfully for the presidency three times. He was known as the "Great Pacificator" for his skill in brokering compromises.

Lyman Hall (April 12, 1724 — October 19, 1790)

Georgia representative Lyman Hall was a signer of the Declaration of Independence and the namesake of Hall County, Georgia.

Religion

John Hagee (April 12, 1940 —)

Televangelist John Hagee is pastor of the 19,000 member Cornerstone Church in San Antonio and the host of a national radio and television ministry. He has been involved in several controversies involving his beliefs and comments.

Science and Mathematics

Peter Safar (April 12, 1924 — August 2, 2003)

Austrian physician Safar .developed the technique of cardiopulmonary resuscitation (CPR), and designed the CPR dummy as well as the method of teaching it.

Ferdinand von Lindemann (April 12, 1852 — March 6, 1939)

German mathematician Lindemann is best known for his proof that pi (π) is a transcendental number, demonstrating that it was impossible to square the circle by compass and straightedge.

Germinal Pierre Dandelin (April 12, 1794 — February 15, 1847)

Belgian mathematician and engineer Pierre Dandelin's contributions include Dandelin spheres, Dandelin's Theorem, and the Dandelin-Gräffe methods of solving algebraic equations.

Sports

Ted Ginn, Jr. (April 12, 1985 —)

Wide receiver Ginn played for the Carolina Panthers, San Francisco 49ers, and the Miami Dolphins. *USA Today* named him Defensive Player of the Year in 2003.

Brennan Boesch (April 12, 1985 —)

Right fielder Boesch has played for the New York Yankees and Detroit Tigers.

Brad Miller (April 12, 1976 —)

Basketball center Miller was a two time NBA All-Star.

Sylvinho (April 12, 1974 —)

Sylvinho was a Brazilian footballer (soccer player) who played in Brazil, Spain, and Great Britain.

Roman Hamrlík (April 12, 1974 —)

Ice hockey defenceman Hamrlík was the first overall pick in the 1992 NHL draft and led the NHL in games played.

Paul Lo Duca (April 12, 1972 —)

MLB catcher Lo Duca played professionally from 1998 to 2008, and subsequently became a horse race analyst.

Sylvain Bouchard (April 12, 1970 —)

Speed skater Bouchard set world records in the 1000m event in 1995 and again in 1998.

Adam Graves (April 12, 1687 —)

NHL left wing Graves played for the New York Rangers, Detroit Red wings, and Edmonton Oilers, with a career record of 329 goals and 287 assists.

Charles Mann (April 12, 1961 —)

NFL defensive end Charles Mann played for the Washington Redskins and San Francisco 49ers. He appeared in three Super Bowls.

Woody Johnson (April 12, 1947 —)

Businessman Woody Johnson bought the New York Jets for $635 million in 2000.

Joe Bowman (April 12, 1925 — June 29,2009)

Marksman Joe "The Straight Shooter," Bowman's pistol and rifle performance included such tricks as shooting a bullet at an axe blade so that the bullet would split and each half would put out a nearby candle. He was a bootmaker by profession, with clients including Roy Rogers, and designed custom holsters for Sammy Davis, Jr. He advised Robert Duvall during the making of *Lonesome Dove*. He is in the Texas Heroes Hall of Honor.

Joe Bowman

Who Died on April 12?

Arts, Film, and Literature

Marilyn Chambers (April 22, 1952 — April 12, 2009)

Former Ivory Snow model Marilyn Chambers was known for her 1972 pornographic film *Behind the Green Door*. She also appeared in some mainstream films, most notably the horror film *Rabid*.

Harvey Ball (July 10, 1921 — April 12, 2001)

Commercial artist Harvey Ball is credited as the earliest known designer of the "smiley" icon.

The "Smiley"

Alan Paton (January 11, 1903 — April 12, 1988)

South African anti-apartheid activist and author Alan Paton is particularly known for his 1948 best-selling novel *Cry, the Beloved Country.*

Medicine

Clara Barton (December 25, 1821 — April 12, 1912)

Civil War nurse Clara Barton (left), known as the "Angel of the Battlefield," first learned of the Red Cross while in Switzerland, and subsequently persuaded the U.S. government to support the establishment of the American Red Cross. Her home, a historic site in Glen Echo, Maryland, preserves the early history of the Red Cross.

Music and Dance

Josephine Baker (June 3, 1906 — April 12, 1975)

International musical star Josephine Baker, variously called the "Bronze Venus," the "Black Pearl," and the "Créole Goddess," was the first African-American female to star in a major movie and the first to integrate an American concert hall. She received the Croix de Guerre for helping the French Resistance in

Josephine Baker in her famous "Banana Skirt" costume from the Folies Bergère

World War II, and was a leader on civil rights issues in the United States.

Arthur Freed (September 9, 1894 — April 12, 1973)

Hollywood producer and lyricist Arthur Freed produced such films as *Babes in Arms, Singin' in the Rain, Show Boat, An American in Paris,* and *Gigi.*

Politics

Abbie Hoffman (November 30, 1936 — April 12, 1989)

Sixties icon Abbie Hoffman co-founded the Youth International Party ("Yippies") and was arrested for his role in violent confrontations between police and demonstrators during the 1968 Democratic National Convention. He and his co-defendants were popularly known as the "Chicago Seven."

Boss Tweed (April 3, 1823 — April 12, 1878)

William Magear "Boss" Tweed was the head of the Tammany Hall political machine, a powerful force in 19th century politics in New York City and State. He was eventually convicted in 1877 of stealing at least $25 million, the equivalent of $1 billion today, and died in jail.

Caricature of Boss Tweed by political cartoonist Thomas Nast

Religion

William Sloane Coffin (June 1, 1924 — April 12, 2006)

Rev. William Sloane Coffin was a liberal American clergyman who became a leader in the civil rights and peace movements of the 1960s and 1970s. He was chaplain of Yale University from the early 1960s to 1975, and subsequently became senior minister at Riverside Church in New York. He and his protégé Rev. Scotty McLennan were the models for the *Doonesbury* character "Rev. Scott Sloan."

Science

Charles Messier (June 26, 1730 — April 12, 1817)

French astronomer Charles Messier (left) is best known for his astronomical catalog of nebulae and star clusters, known as "Messier objects," which provided a numbering system still in use. A crater on the Moon and an asteroid are named for him.

Sports

Sugar Ray Robinson (May 3, 1921 — April 12, 1989)

Boxer Sugar Ray Robinson was both Welterweight Champion and Middleweight Champion of the World. Sportswriters have ranked him "pound for pound" as the greatest boxer of all time.

Sugar Ray Robinson

Joe Louis (May 13, 1914 — April 12, 1981)

Nicknamed the "Brown Bomber," World Heavyweight Champion boxer Joe Louis is ranked as the #1 heavyweight of all time by the International Boxing Research Organization. He enlisted during World War II as a private and was used as a focus for recruiting drives.

Joe Lewis during his World War II Army service

Ed Lafitte (April 7, 1886 — April 12, 1971)

MLB pitcher Ed Lafitte played in the major leagues from 1909 to 1915, and subsequently became a dentist for 42 years.

April
The Fourth Month

"I love the season well
When forest glades are teeming with bright forms,
Nor dark and many-folded clouds foretell
The coming on of storms."

— *"An April Day," Henry Wadsworth Longfellow*

The origin of the name "April" (Latin: *Aprilis*) for the fourth month of the year is uncertain. Some say that it comes from the Latin verb *aperire*, meaning "to open," a reference to springtime. A similar word in Greek, ἄνοιξις (*anoixis*), meaning "opening" also refers to spring.

On the other hand, the Romans named many months after their gods, such as "January" for Janus and "March" (*Martius*) for Mars. The month of April was sacred to the goddess Venus (*Aphrodite* in Greek), and thus some think that April refers to her.

The fairy tale collector Jacob Grimm suggested that April came from the Etruscan name *Apru*, and believed that an Etruscan god or hero of that name gave rise to the month.

As the original Roman calendar started its new year in March, April was originally the second month of the year. It's uncertain when the Romans switched the new year to January, but it may have been as late as 153 BCE.

April is the springtime month in the northern hemisphere and fall in the southern hemisphere; October is its opposite. It's one of only four calendar months with thirty days. Originally, April had only 29 days, but the calendar reforms of Julius Caesar (the Julian Calendar) added the 30th day.

The first day of April and the first day of July always fall on the same day of the week; in leap years the first of January also falls on the same weekday as the first of April. In all years, the last day of April and the last day of December fall on the same wekday.

April in Other Cultures

The Anglo-Saxons called April *Oster-monath*, sometimes spelled *Eostur-monath*, named for the goddess *Eostre*. The Venerable Bede, a monk who wrote the first history of the English people, argued that Eostur was the root of the word Easter.

In China, the Emperor and princes of the blood would symbolically plow the earth to get ready for the planting season. This took place in their third month, sān yuè (三月), which most often overlaps with April in their traditional lunisolar calendar.

In Finland, March is called *huhtikuu* (burnwood month), representing the clearing of farmland. In Slovene, the traditional name is *mali traven* (the months when plants start growing). In Hebrew, Arabic, and modern Turkish, the month of *Nisan* (Hebrew: נִיסָן ; Arabic: نيسان) overlaps March and April. It comes from a Sumerian word, *nisag*, meaning "first fruits."

April Symbols

Birthstone: Diamond

Birth Flowers: Daisy and Sweet Pea

Daisy

Sweet Pea

April Events

Honorary Months

Presidents, Congresses, and nations around the world issue proclamations recognizing particular months to honor certain causes. These events generally fall in April. (All US unless otherwise noted.)

- Autism Awareness Month
- Confederate History Month (southern United States)
- Financial Literacy Month
- Jazz Appreciation Month
- National Arab-American Heritage Month
- National Child Abuse Prevention Month
- National Poetry Month
- Parkinson's Disease Awareness Month (International)

Moveable and Multi-Day Events

Some events take place over a specific week or time period. Start and finish dates may vary from year to year. Some events occur on different days each year (such as "fourth Saturday of a month"). The events of Easter season are part of this category, but the number of the events are such that Easter receives its own separate section.

International Trombone Week

Sponsored by the International Trombone Association, International Trombone Week took place on April 7-14 in 2013, and April 1-15 in 2012. Numerous recitals, concerts, and symposia take place around the world celebrating the trombone. (www.trombone.net)

Passover (פסח) (Judaism, Samaritanism, Saint Thomas Christians)

Passover commemorates the liberation of the Israelites from slavery in ancient Egypt around 3,300 years ago. Its story is told in the Biblical book of Exodus, which is part of both the Jewish and Samaritan Torahs and the Christian Old Testament. Exodus tells how God inflicted ten plagues upon the ancient Egyptians before the Pharaoh would release its slaves. The tenth plague killed every Egyptian first-born child. Israelites marked the doorposts of their homes with the blood of a spring lamb so that the spirit of the Lord would "pass over" the first-born in those homes. Passover is celebrated by Jews in a festive ritual dinner known as a Seder and by Samaritans with an animal sacrifice on Mount Gerizim.

For most celebrants, Passover begins on the 15th day of Nisan and ends on the 21st of Nisan in Israel and on the 22nd of Nisan outside of Israel. The earliest dates for Passover are between March 21 and March 27 (or 28), and the latest dates fall between April 20 and April 26 (or 27).

Opening Day (Major League Baseball)

Major League Baseball generally begins its annual season on the first Monday in April (although it has been moved to different days to keep the World Series from extending into November).

President Woodrow Wilson throws the Opening Day pitch, 1916

Easter Events

La crucifixión by El Greco

Easter Season

The Christian holiday of Easter in Western Christianity is held on the first Sunday after the Paschal Full Moon following the March equinox, which is officially set at March 21 by church reckoning. Easter itself can therefore occur as early as March 22 and as late as April 25, but occurs most often in April. In Eastern Christianity, which uses the Julian calendar, Easter occurs between April 4 and May 8. This also sets the date for the various events that lead up to Easter, most importantly the events of Holy Week.

Passion Sunday

The fifth Sunday of the Christian season of Lent is known as Passion Sunday in various Protestant denominations and by some traditionalist Catholics. Sometimes, the sixth Sunday of Lent is referred to as Passion Sunday, but it is more commonly known as Palm Sunday.

Passion Sunday starts the two-week Passiontide, which ends on Holy Saturday, the day before Easter, commemorating the day that Jesus's body was laid in the tomb. The fifth Sunday of Lent can occur as early as March 8 (though the next time it will be that early is in 2285 CE), and as late as April 11.

Palm Sunday

The moveable feast of Palm Sunday commemorates the triumphant entry of Jesus into Jerusalem, an event mentioned in all four gospels. In many Christian churches, palm leaves are distributed to the worshippers. The earliest date for Palm Sunday is March 15, and the latest is April 18.

Maundy Thursday

The Thursday before Easter is Maundy Thursday, when the Last Supper took place. The earliest day it can occur is March 19, and the latest is April 22.

Good Friday

Good Friday, observed during Holy Week on the Friday preceding Easter Sunday, commemorates the crucifixion of Jesus and his death at Calvary. The earliest day it can occur is March 20, and the latest is April 23.

Holy Saturday

Sometimes called Easter Eve or Black Saturday, Holy Saturday commemorates the day in which Jesus's body lay in the tomb. Some mistakenly refer to this day as "Easter Saturday," but that properly describes the Saturday following Easter, the last day of Easter Week. The earliest it can occur is March 21, and the latest is April 24.

Easter Eggs

Easter

Easter celebrates the resurrection of Jesus Christ on the third day after his crucifixion.

In the liturgical calendar, Easter follows the season of Lent, and begins the period known as Eastertide, which ends on Pentecost Sunday. Easter is observed religiously in a morning service.

In the U.S., it's also common to decorate Easter eggs and make Easter baskets of eggs and candy, often with the Easter bunny as a symbol. The White House traditionally hosts an egg hunt, and many communities have Easter parades.

Easter customs around the world include bonfires (Cyprus, western Sweden), men spanking women with a ceremonial whip (Czech Republic and Slovakia), egg fighting (Bulgaria), cross-country skiing and reading murder mysteries (Norway), and children dressed as witches collecting candy door-to-door (other Nordic countries).

Easter Monday

In some Roman Catholic and Eastern Orthodox cultures, the Monday after Easter is celebrated as a holiday.

It is also known in some countries as **Egg Nyte**, featuring egg rolling competitions and dousing other people with water that had been blessed with holy water the previous day at mass.

Easter Monday is also celebrated as **Family Day** in South Africa. In Guyana, people fly kites that were made on Holy Saturday. In Portugal, it is known as the **Anjo (Ivy) Festival**, in which people picnic in the countryside.

Śmigus-Dyngus (Poland, Hungary, Czech Republic, Slovakia)

The Monday after Easter in Poland and in the Polish diaspora is known as *Śmigus-Dyngus*, or simply Dyngus Day in the US. Boys throw water over girls they like and spank them with pussy willows. Girls avoid getting wet by giving boys "ransoms" of painted eggs.

Easter Week (Western Christianity)
Bright Week (Eastern Christianity)

The period from Easter Sunday to the following Saturday is known as **Easter Week**. In both Western and Eastern Christianity (where it's known as **Bright Week**), the resurrection continues to be celebrated in church services. **Easter Tuesday** is a public holiday in the Australian state of Tasmania. Because of the difference in the calculation of the date of Easter, Easter Week and Bright Week happen on different weeks each year.

A Bright Week procession

March Zodiac Signs

From the perspective of someone on Earth, the Sun appears to move through the sky throughout the year, along a path astronomers call the ecliptic plane. The ecliptic plane is divided into twelve constellations, known as the zodiac, based on traditionally observed patterns of stars. On your birthday, you can't see your constellation, because it's part of the daytime sky.

The zodiac was first developed by Babylonian astronomers about 2,500 years ago. Because they were unaware that the Earth wobbles like a spinning top (a motion known as *precession*), they didn't make allowance for the fact that the Sun's path through the zodiac changes over time.

That means there are now two sets of dates for your birth sign. The *tropical* dates are the original Babylonian dates; the *siderial* dates tell you where the Sun actually appears as it moves along its annual path.

In siderial reckoning, April 12 is in Pisces, but in tropical astrology, April 12 is in Aries.

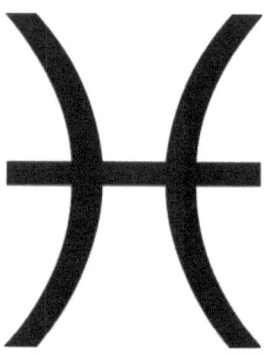

Pisces

Tropical February 20 to March 20

Siderial March 15 to April 14

In the Roman legend of Venus and her son Cupid, they escaped the clutches of Typhon, known as the "father of all monsters," by transforming into fish and tying themselves together with rope. That's why the name Pisces is plural for fish. The constellation appears as a somewhat ragged "V" shape, representing the rope, with the "fish" located at the two rope ends.

In astrology, Pisces is a water sign, compatible with the other water signs Cancer and Scorpio, as well as with the earth signs Taurus, Virgo, and Capricorn. Pisceans are supposed to be imaginative, compassionate, unworldly, secretive, and escapist.

Aries

Tropical March 21 to April 19

Siderial April 15 to May 15

In Greek mythology, Aries is a ram with golden wings and golden wool who rescued the twins Phrixus and Helle from certain death. Although Helle died in the rescue attempt, the grateful Phrixus sacrificed the ram to Zeus. The golden fleece from the sacrificed ram played a prominent part in the later myth of Jason and the Argonauts.

In astrology, Aries, a fire sign, is compatible with the other fire signs of Gemini, Leo, and Sagittarius, and to a lesser extent with air signs Scorpio and Libra. Arians are supposed to be adventurous, enthusiastic, quick-tempered, and impulsive.

Illustration by Edward Penfield

What Day of the Week is April 11?

On what day of the week does April 11 fall?

Surprisingly, this isn't an easy question. Because the calendar year is 365 days long (366 in leap years), it doesn't divide evenly by the seven days of the week.

Also, the Earth goes around the Sun in about 365-1/4 days, so a calendar tends to drift over time. That's why the same date falls on different weekdays in different years.

This is made even more complicated by a change in calendars that took place in 1582. Our modern calendar has its roots in ancient Rome, in a calendar reform conducted by Julius Caesar. Caesar commissioned mathematicians to attack the problem, and came up with the idea of *leap years,* and thus standardized the calendar for centuries to come. This was called the *Julian calendar.*

Over time, however, the small errors in Caesar's calculation compounded. That's why Pope Gregory XIII commissioned the *Gregorian calendar,* used in most of the world today. Some countries converted in 1582, when the calendar was first developed; some converted later; other still haven't changed.

Gregorian and Julian aren't the only types of calendars. The Hebrew year, the Islamic year, and many other calendars are used in different parts of the world and among different people.

You can convert Gregorian dates to other calendars, including the Hebrew calendar, the Islamic calendar, and even the Mayan calendar by visiting the Fourmilab Calendar Converter at http://www.fourmilab.ch/documents/calendar/.

Chinese calendar systems are quite complex and have changed several times; a full discussion is far beyond the scope of this book. If you're interested, you can find information here: http://www.hermetic.ch/cal_stud/chinese_cal.htm.

A 50-year brass perpetual calendar.

Copyright, Credit, and Contact

Follow Us

Our blog Dobson's Improbable History features short articles on events and people associated with each day, and updates several times each week. Get the latest on Twitter @SidewiseThinker.

Contact Us

Find an error or a format problem? Want information about the series, about us, or about when the volume for your special day might be available? Please email us at editor@timespinnerpress.com.

On Dates

Historians use "CE" (Common Era) and "BCE" (Before the Common Era) instead of the more common "AD" (*Anno Domini*, or Year of Our Lord) and "BC" (Before Christ), reflecting the fact that the year-numbering system established by the Gregorian calendar is used throughout the world in many countries not culturally Christian. The CE/BCE designation dates back to at least 1708, and have been adopted as a standard by the United Nations and the Universal Postal Union. Because this series of books covers events and people of all nations and cultures, we use the CE/BCE terms.

The abbreviation "O.S." on some dates refers to the fact that the Russian Empire did not switch from the Julian to the Gregorian calendar at the same time as the rest of Europe, and therefore some figures and events have two dates.

People and events whose original names are not in the Western alphabet have their native names (where possible) in the appropriate script shown in parenthesis. If you are using an e-reader to access an electronic version of this book, all characters don't always display on all devices.

Sources and Art Credits

We owe a great debt to Wikipedia, which is our first stop for research. We attempt to make independent confirmation of all important dates and facts through a variety of other sources. Other sources we frequently use include the Library of Congress; "on this day" listings from *Encyclopedia Britannica*, the New York *Times*, and the BBC; and, of course, the always-useful Google.

All art and photographs are either in the public domain, used under a Creative Commons license, or with a "fair use" justification, and most frequently come from Wikimedia Commons and the Library of Congress Prints and Photographs Division.

Attribution is provided where requested by the copyright owner or when of historical significance, listed below. For information about any particular illustration or photograph, please contact us.

- The photograph of the Late Show marquee was taken by "Hey Paul" from State College, Pennsylvania, and is used here under the CC BY-2.0 license.

- The publicity photograph of Tiny Tim on *Rowan & Martin's Laugh-In* is in the public domain because it was published in the United States between 1923 and 1977 without a copyright notice.

- The publicity photograph of Lily Pons is in the public domain because it was published in the United States between 1923 and 1963, and if it was copyrighted, the copyright was not renewed.

- The 1842 portrait of Henry Clay by John Neagle is in the public domain because its copyright has expired. The original is in the Smithsonian Institution's National Portrait Gallery in Washington, DC.

- The publicity photograph of Joe Bowman was released into the public domain by the copyright holder.

- The generic smiley face illustration was released into the public domain by the artist.

- The photograph of Clara Barton is in the public domain as a work of the U.S. federal government.

- The 1927 photograph of Josephine Baker in Banana Skirt from the Folies Bergère is in the public domain because its copyright has expired.

- The Boss Tweed political cartoon by Thomas Nast was published before 1871 and is in the public domain because its copyright has expired.

- The portrait of Charles Messier is by Ansiaume, circa 1770, and is in the public domain because its copyright has expired.

- The 1965 photograph of Sugar Ray Robinson is a work for hire created prior to 1968 by a staff photographer at New York *World-Telegram & Sun*. It is part of a collection donated to the Library of Congress. Per the deed of gift, New York World-Telegram & Sun dedicated to the public all rights it held for the photographs in this collection.

- The 1943 cartoon of Sgt. Joe Louis is by Charles Alston for the Office of War Information and is in the public domain as a work of the U.S. federal government.

- The photograph of two diamonds grown by Washington Diamonds was taken by Inbai-Tania Studio, and is used here under the CC BY-SA 3.0 license.

- The photograph of a daisy (*Bellis perennis*) was taken by André Karwath and is used here under the CC BY-SA 2.5 license.

- The photograph of President Woodrow Wilson throwing the ball on the opening day of baseball season 1916 is a press photograph from the National Photo Company Collection, part of the Library of Congress Prints and Photographs Division, and is in the public domain because it was published prior to January 1, 1923.

- The painting *La crucifixión* by El Greco is located in the Museo del Prado. It is in the public domain because its copyright has expired.

- The photograph of Czechoslovakian Easter eggs was taken by Jan Kameníček, who has released the image into the public domain.

- The 1988 photograph of a Bright Week procession is by George Rassasphore and is used here under the CC BY-SA 1.0 license.

- The photograph of the 1906 automobile calendar by Edward Penfield is from the Library of Congress Prints and Photographs Division, and is in the public domain because it was published prior to January 1, 1923.

- The 50-year perpetual calendar photograph is in the public domain.

License Description and Terms

Aside from material purely in the public domain, photographs and other material in this book are used under specific licenses permitting free use, usually with attribution. For full text and terms of these licenses, click or enter the appropriate links below.

Creative Commons Attribution 2.0 Generic (CC BY 2.0):: http:// creativecommons.org/licenses/by/2.0/deed.en

Timespinner
Press